CHIARA LUCE

A life lived to the full

CHIARA LUCE
A life lived to the full

Michele Zanzucchi

New City Press
Hyde Park, NY

Published in the United States by New City Press
202 Comforter Blvd., Hyde Park, NY 12538
www.newcitypress.com

First published in Italy as *Io ho tutto*
by Città Nuova, Rome, Italy
© Città Nuova, Rome 2004

First published in Great Britain by New City
Unit 17
Sovereign Park
Coronation Road
London NW10 7QP
© New City, London 2007

Translated by Frank Johnson
Cover design by Tomeu Mayans

British Cataloguing in Publication Data:
A catalogue reference for this book is available from
the British Library

ISBN 978 0 904287 98 1

Typeset in Great Britain by
New City, London

Printed in the United States of America

CONTENTS

CHAPTER 1

BEGINNINGS

It's a fact that Pope John Paul II has created more saints than all the other popes in history put together. And it's a fact that after the Second Vatican Council, the concept of sanctity has widened, as can be seen from the large number of married people, fathers and mothers, who have been beatified. Nevertheless it still comes as something of a surprise to us that an apparently ordinary 18-year old girl was able, in just a short time, to arrive at heaven's door. Where did she find the strength to refuse the morphine offered to her by her doctors to relieve the pain of the advancing cancer? She said that she still wanted to be able "to offer something". Normally, the passing of a young person would be marked by some tears, a few lines in the local paper and comments like "poor girl, and so young too". But still, years after her death, Chiara Badano is not just remembered – she is taken as a model of sanctity by thousands of young people all over the world. So, the question is: "How could a girl reach such a depth of spiritual life in such a brief period of time?"

As I write this, I am looking at one of the last photographs of Chiara, taken as she lay, paralysed, on her bed, in her home in Sassello. She is covered with a tartan blanket and is looking directly at the camera, her arm behind her head. Her head is covered by a thin covering of dark hair, not the latest style, but evidence of the chemotherapy she had been undergoing. And yet her face betrays nothing of a gravely ill person on the point of death, rather it is the face of a young girl who has come to maturity in a short period of time. She is smiling. It is a smile that so many had come to love. But above all it is those two big eyes which gave witness, and on which my gaze remained fixed. They are serene and sincere, and they express everything Chiara believed in and lived for. They are eyes which know that "medicine has laid down its arms", but also that "love conquers everything". With her, in the room, in that moment, were three friends from Genoa. They had been chatting with Chiara, living another of those moments of the Gospel "in action" which she so loved. "Moments of unity," she called them. This is Chiara Badano, or rather, Chiara Luce.

Not icons, but models

Every social group has its models in whom its hopes and aspirations are personified. The Gen Movement, the young people of the Focolare Movement, has, ever since the 1960s, been very close to its members as they got ready to "go to heaven". There is Francesco Chiarati, for example, a young lad from Brescia in Italy, and Charles Moates, murdered in Chicago, whose story has been

8

made into a musical by Gen Rosso. Then there are the Gen girls from Pelotas in Brazil, who were killed in a road accident on their way to a Gen congress... Each generation has its stories of heroism and sanctity, which then become models for those coming after them. And yet these young people who have gone to the next life were not aloof or idealised; they have not become "icons", to use the current terminology. They were just going on ahead of the others to another place, where they all eventually hope to meet up again.

The Church has always spoken about the "communion of saints", a rather obscure expression perhaps, which is often thought of as something remote, something that exists only up in heaven. But among the Gen the communion of saints has always been something real, something that brings heaven and earth closer together.

This might give us a key into the interest in the life of Chiara Luce even before she left this earth. Just as with other friends who were ill, or perhaps more so, the Gen wanted to know the latest on her health which came to them on their informal network. They also prayed, and how! They saw in her someone for whom God had a special love.

Then, when she died, the news spread quickly, and some of her writings began to circulate. People still talk about the funeral as a "wedding feast". In the years that followed, without any particular pattern, thanks to a collection of her writings, a biography and a video, and through her friends, the local bishop and the Gen, Chiara Luce's life continues to inspire people.

Sassello

From Savona follow the coast road down to Albisola and then turn inland for twenty kilometres or so, up a narrow, winding road to Sassello, a village of less than two thousand inhabitants, some 60 kilometres from the great maritime city of Genoa. During the week many of the houses in Sassello are empty, only to be filled at weekends and during the summer months by their city-dwelling owners. North and South meet on the surrounding mountains, which means that there is no shortage of rain and snow in the winter months. Sassello is a picturesque mountain village whose territory takes in the 1,287-metre-high Mt Beigua. Once renowned throughout Italy for its chestnuts, many of its trees were destroyed by a disease that infested the woods around Sassello between the wars. Nowadays it is famous for its fine mushrooms, a much-sought-after delicacy in kitchens and restaurants around Italy. But Sassello is best known for its "amaretti", a kind of biscuit, produced in six different factories around the village, whose recipes are closely guarded secrets, passed on from one generation to the next.

Sassello was where Chiara Badano was born and died. She loved Sassello, and whenever she had had to stay over in Savona, she was always delighted to come home again after her period of "exile" in the big city.

A united family

In Sassello practically half the population has the surname Badano. In fact, there is a village nearby which is called Badani, and Ruggero Badano lives in Via Badano! Ruggero started work in the family shop, selling fabrics, but later he started his own one-man business, driving a lorry. Maria Teresa Caviglia came from a poor family, with seven brothers and sisters. They became even poorer when the family home was destroyed in a fire, and only the charity of the neighbours helped them survive through the severe winter that followed.

Maria Teresa and Ruggero were at nursery school together. But after that they did not meet one another very much, except in the local church on special feast days. "She loved dancing," explained Ruggero, "but I didn't, so we moved in different circles." She got engaged to a local lad and that was that, or so it seemed. But Ruggero had other ideas: "Maria Teresa was my first love," he said, "And it stayed that way. But at that time I just couldn't bring myself to declare my feelings for her, until eventually it became obvious to her..."

The fact was, he was a man of few words, but with a strong faith. He was pretty serious, but he had a gentle look in his eyes that made him everybody's friend. Maria Teresa, on the other hand, was affable and extroverted, gentle yet determined.

The community of Sassello

In a small village the parish has a key role in forming the basic attitudes and opinions of the population. The community of Sassello could certainly be called "solidly traditional". Still today, there is quite a high percentage of churchgoers. Every year, on the feast of Corpus Christi, the streets of Sassello are decorated with huge arrangements of flowers and the walls of the houses along the route of the procession are covered with chestnut tree branches.

On Good Friday there is a solemn procession through the village where members of the ancient confraternities (all men), on their knees, accompany a huge wooden cross up to the "hill of Calvary", while singing laments in Latin. And all around the area there are numerous votive chapels, each with its own feast day. The villagers join in all these festivities, often attracted by the external features such as the choirs, the theatrical productions, the fritters or the chestnut cakes. But something deeper is communicated all the same.

One of Maria Teresa's childhood memories shows the social importance of the parish and its influence on the people. "In our church there was the custom of reserving the first few rows of benches for the families of benefactors," she said. "For my first communion I sat down, as usual, at the back. But the parish priest came down from the altar, took me by the hand and led me to the front. He also gave me the banner to carry in the procession."

"I couldn't believe it..."

Maria Teresa and Ruggero had been married ten years, and had not been able to have any children. "I considered everything that happened to me to be the will of God," said Maria Teresa. "He loved me, and so this inability to have children was love too." Ruggero's view was rather different, however. "All my friends had plenty of children, and we had none. I really felt that we were missing out," he said.

The decisive moment came when Ruggero went to visit the shrine at Rocche. His prayer asking for a child was deeply sincere and one month later Maria Teresa became pregnant. She was already 37. "I just couldn't believe it," she said, "I didn't tell anyone I was pregnant and tried to rest as much as possible, because the doctor had explained that it would be three weeks or so before we would have confirmation. That day Ruggero could not contain his joy and he began to speak about 'our pregnancy'."

The new father-to-be didn't want to take any risks with the pregnancy and so he did everything possible to help Maria Teresa rest. He even used to carry her upstairs in his arms. "My love for my wife moved on to another plane over those nine months," he explained, "But so did my love for the Lord."

Chiara was born, by forceps delivery, on 29 October 1971. "From happiness I went into shock, " said Maria Teresa, "For 24 hours it was like living in a dream. I kept asking myself if my baby really had been born, because they didn't let me see her... Then eventually I saw that little bundle of a baby and my heart was filled with joy. But at the same time as feeling this immense joy, we both realised that, in the first place, that baby was a child of God."

Childhood experiences

Chiara had a carefree, serene childhood. She was the sort of child every mother wants – even-tempered, a good sleeper and, when she did wake early, she played on her own with her toys. In these early days Maria Teresa became ill with phlebitis and had to spend three months in bed. Her sister came to help, but Maria Teresa would not delegate the care of her daughter to anyone else. She had given up her job. "I had always worked in the biscuit factory," she said, "and was afraid of being bored by housework. But I soon realised how important it is to be with your own child, not so much talking, but 'being' a mother, in other words, loving. This was the only legacy that I could leave her: to teach her to love."

She didn't think twice about taking her to church, "so that she got used to it", and even though she still hadn't reached the so-called age of reason, Maria Teresa used to whisper in her ear the story of Jesus and Mary. And the child listened without disturbing any of the people near them, dressed in her warm pink baby suit, because it was winter and the snow was deeper than usual that year.

From an early age Chiara was generous. In her first year at primary school she wrote to Baby Jesus and asked, not for toys, but simply that "Grandma Gilda and all those who are ill should be made better". And if ever there was any disagreement with her parents, she never let more than a few moments pass before she made it up with them.

One day, for example, Maria Teresa had asked Chiara to help clear the table. "I don't want to," she replied, folding her arms across her chest, and marching off towards her room. But she didn't even get that far, because in just a few seconds she turned back saying, "How does that story from the Gospel go, the one about the father who asks his son to go the vineyard, whereas the other said no and then went there? Mummy, put my apron on." And she set about clearing the table.

On another occasion, Maria Teresa, seeing that there were perhaps too many toys in Chiara's room, invited her to give some of them to the poor children. Chiara said no, that they were her toys. Maria Teresa left her, but almost immediately she heard a noise coming from Chiara's room. She stood outside the door and listened: "This one yes, that one no. This one yes..." When Maria Teresa pushed open the door, there was Chiara selecting which toys to give away and which to keep. When her mother asked her how she made the selection, Chiara replied: "I can't give broken toys to children who don't have any."

An education in common sense

Being the only child of older parents and the centre of attention for the wider family, there was a real danger of Chiara being spoilt. "We were aware of this danger," said Maria Teresa, "so, right from the beginning we wanted to be clear with Chiara. We often reminded her that she had a father in heaven who was much greater than us two." An original way of stopping her from throwing tantrums...

The "educational model" chosen by Ruggero and Maria Teresa did not come from books; it was inherited from healthy, united families, as well as from the life of a good, solid parish. But above all it was an education built on the love between the parents. One example of this "method" of education can be seen in something that happened when Chiara was four. Maria Teresa suggested that Chiara should say her prayers. Chiara replied that she had other things to do. The mother could have insisted, but she remembered that, in the first place, Chiara was God's child and that he had given her the gift of free will, which had to be respected. So, she said that she would say the prayers herself on Chiara's behalf. She started to say the prayer to the guardian angel and, a few seconds later, she heard Chiara repeating her words. "It was a very important lesson for me," said Maria Teresa, "One of those which I won't easily forget. Yes, it was my duty to educate her, but first if all I had to pass love on to her."

Ruggero played a "strong" role in Chiara's upbringing. "By nature, I was rather strict," he explained, "and I felt that I had to be quite insistent with Chiara; but I always did it out of love, always; never out of spite, or tiredness, or for any other reason. So, Chiara grew up with a similar character to mine..." "Yes," agreed Maria Teresa, "but we never expected 'blind' obedience from her. She had a right to express her point of view, but the relationship had to be in the truth. Lies were never tolerated."

Maria Teresa gave an example of this when she recounted one particular incident: "One afternoon Chiara arrived home with a lovely red apple. I asked where she had got it. She said that she had got it from Gianna, the owner of the beautiful old mill below our house. But she hadn't asked permission, so I told her that she should ask for things before taking them and that she must take it back immediately and apologise to our neighbour. She didn't want to; she was too ashamed. I explained to her that the truth was more important than eating a nice apple. After a moment's hesitation, Chiara (followed by me, with a reassuring smile) went to see Gianna and told her the tale. A little later there was a knock at the door, and there was Gianna with a whole basket of apples for Chiara, 'because today she has learnt a very important lesson'."

CHAPTER 2

DISCOVERING AN IDEAL

When Chiara was just eight years old she came across something that seemed made just for her: it was the Focolare Movement. She heard about it from some of her friends, about this great ideal, which could transform the life of whoever chose to live it. She went to her first Focolare meeting in September 1980 where she discovered a new way of living and thinking, something which satisfied her thirst for God. From that moment on, Chiara was never the same again.

A short time later, her parents also met the Movement when they attended an international congress on the family, Familyfest, in Rome in 1981. Ruggero explained the impact his meeting the Focolare had: "I didn't really feel like going to Rome," he said, "but I decided to go to give the family a chance to see the capital city. We spent three days looking round Rome, but when it was time to go to the Familyfest I started to drag my feet. So, we arrived late and people had to make room for us in that crowded sports arena. I heard a few words from the stage: they were speaking about a kind of love that was different from the love I had for Maria Teresa and for Chiara, a love that was strong and both natural and supernatural. Gradually it dawned on me that there was a Jesus right next to me, to whom I could speak personally, to whom I could tell everything. I 'capitulated' when Chiara said she was hungry and straightaway the people next to us offered her a sandwich, some fruit and a drink. And at lunch time, even though we had brought our own food, we only ate the food that was offered to us."

"When we got back home," said Maria Teresa, "if someone had asked us when we were married, we would have said: 'When we met this Ideal'." "At last," continued Ruggero, "I had understood that this Jesus was near me; I felt his presence very strongly. Then, when I came across a difficulty, perhaps because of my own boorishness, I felt as if I couldn't breathe properly. Something wasn't quite right, but I didn't know what. Then I realised what it was: if I stopped loving, there was something missing in the relationship – I needed the 'other lung' to be able to breathe well."

From that moment, the Badanos were even more an example of respect, warmth and unity than they had been previously. But this witness of unity was to become even more evident a few years later when Chiara fell ill.

Where Chiara left her heart

Chiara was linked to the Gen 3 group, first in Albisola and then in Genoa. They played a lot and they certainly enjoyed themselves, but there was more to it than that.

At Chiara's first meeting with the Gen 3, on 29 September 1980, they wrote the following: "We started our adventure straightaway: to do the will of God in the present moment. With the Gospel in our hands we will do great things."

A friend of Chiara's at that time, Lucia, said: "We played and we invented all sorts of fun. Chiara was full of life, a real live wire and a great one to have as a friend. Her happiness infected everyone. She always had a smile on her face and a pure look in her eyes. Her greatest asset was her vitality."

On 29 August that year, Chiara wrote her first letter to Chiara Lubich, the founder of the Focolare. She wrote: "Dear Chiara Lubich, first of all let me introduce myself. I am a girl who is nearly ten and my name is Chiara too. I live in a little village called Sassello in the province of Savona. I know you because on 3 May I went to the family congress in Rome with my parents, and in the middle of that huge crowd of people I managed to see you through the binoculars. This year I was fortunate enough to take part in my first Mariapolis. I didn't go with my parents, but chose instead to go with the Gen 3. It was held at a beautiful shrine called the Madonna del Pozzo. When my mum left me there I was a bit worried, and she said to me: 'Now Chiara, you're on your own. Try to behave yourself.' But I replied: 'Mum, I'm not on my own, Jesus is here'. The other girls I met were nice and kind, and different from the ones at school, and together we tried to live for Jesus. I had a little experience too. I lent my shoes to a girl who had to go up on the stage to tell her experience to the adults in the Mariapolis. A great big hug, Chiara."

Certain elements contained in this letter were to develop and grow to maturity very strongly in later years, especially during the two years of her illness: the choice of God and the choice of unity, and the priority given to the Gospel lived.

The way that Chiara distanced herself from her parents with the words: "Mum, I'm not on my own, Jesus is here," is reminiscent of Jesus' reaction when he is found by his parents with the doctors in the temple. Then that "We tried to live for Jesus" shows that, right from the start, she had understood the heart of the spirituality of unity. And finally, the experience about the shoes shows that she understood that either one lives the Gospel or it is just a collection of dead words.

The first choice

So, Chiara, still not 12 years old, continued to be in love with the Gospel. At night, before going to sleep, she would write a few little experiences of the day. In one such writing we find: "One of my schoolmates has got scarlet fever and everyone is scared of visiting her. With my parents' permission I am going to take her her homework, so that she doesn't feel lonely. I believe that love is more important than fear."

In 1983 Chiara went twice to Rocca di Papa, near Rome, where international Gen 3 congresses were held. As usual there was disapproval from grandparents and aunts and uncles, who thought that Ruggero and Maria Teresa should not have let a young girl travel such a long distance without her parents. But it was on occasions such as these that Chiara made her choice very clear.

On 17 June 1983 she wrote the following to Chiara Lubich: "This was my first congress, and I have to say that it was a marvellous experience. I rediscovered Jesus forsaken in a special way. I experienced him in every person that passed by me. This year I have made a new resolution to see Jesus forsaken as my spouse and to welcome him joyfully and, above all, with all the love possible."

A few months later on 27 November, just after her twelfth birthday, she wrote: "The most important thing for me during this congress was the rediscovery of Jesus forsaken. Before, I lived it rather superficially, and I accepted him in order afterwards to feel the joy. In this congress I realised that I had got it all wrong. I shouldn't just exploit him, but love him for himself. I have discovered that Jesus forsaken is the key to unity with God. I want to choose him as my spouse and get ready for when he comes – to prefer him. I have understood that I can find him in those who are far from God, in atheists, and that I have to love him in a very special way, without any self-interest."

Jesus forsaken is one of the main points of the Focolare spirituality of unity. When Jesus cried out on the cross: "My God, my God, why have you forsaken me?" he felt completely cut off from the Father, but at the same moment he repaired the broken unity between God and man. When a member of the Focolare talks about choosing to love Jesus forsaken, they mean that they try to love him in all the difficult circumstances and situations of their lives and the lives of those near them. Jesus forsaken is therefore the key to unity between people on earth, and between heaven and earth. Chiara Badano, at the age of 12, had made the radical decision to put love for Jesus forsaken at the centre of her life.

The two Chiaras – an unbroken link

Chiara Badano began to correspond regularly with Chiara Lubich, founder of the Focolare Movement. This relationship became a vital element in the spiritual journey of the girl from Sassello. After her first Gen 3 congress, aged 11, she wrote: "I can't find words to express my thanks, but I know that I owe everything to you and to God." And at the end of her life she again expressed her gratitude: "I owe everything to God and to Chiara."

In November 1985, just after she had started high school, Chiara wrote: "Dear Mother, during this congress I have rediscovered the Gospel in a new light. I realised that I wasn't an authentic Christian because I wasn't living it fully. Now I want to make this magnificent book [the Gospels] the only aim in my life. I don't want to and I can't remain ignorant of such an extraordinary message. Just as for me it is easy to learn the alphabet, so must I learn to live the Gospel. I have rediscovered the expression: 'Give and it will be given to you'. I must learn to have a greater faith in Jesus, to believe in his immense love. Thank you for the great gift that I always find new every day."

In the Focolare Movement there is a custom, taken from the early Christian communities, for people to take a "new name" when they embark on their new journey of faith. They also like to have a personal "word of life", a sentence from Scripture, to help live the will of God more faithfully. Many of the Gen 3 write directly to Chiara Lubich to ask for a new name and a word of life. In fact, Chiara Badano had written three times asking for a name and a word, but without reply. "Chiara suffered a lot because she had not received a reply to her letters," said Maria Teresa, "The other Gen 3 had got their 'new names', but not Chiara. One day, after the mail had been delivered without anything for her, she said: 'Chiara still hasn't replied. Never mind, she has plenty of things to do... And anyway I've already got everything I need.' I firmly believe that it was all part of God's plan: she had to get ready."

Sport, friendships and the Gospel

St Augustine repeatedly remarked that love makes us beautiful. Chiara was clothed in evangelical beauty; she was pretty, an attractive girl. Photographs of Chiara give the impression of someone who is strong-willed, with a well-defined character. But what strikes you is her gaze. It is neither timid nor aggressive; it is just open and pure.

Chiara's adolesecence did not seem to change her character. She still did the things she had done for years, like visiting the old ladies in the nursing home nearby. One of these ladies, Speranza, was tiny, very reserved, but also very forthright, in every sense of the word. One day, when Chiara went to visit her, Speranza seemed rather sad. Eventually Chiara discovered that it was because someone had been stealing her washing. From that day on, Speranza's clothes were washed at Chiara Badano's house. On another occasion, Speranza wanted to have her feet rested, but she wouldn't let "that girl" do it; so Maria Teresa took the job on.

Another episode involved one of Chiara's friends, Roberta. Roberta's mother was in hospital to have a tumour removed, and Chiara in effect adopted her. Some time later, Roberta's grandmother was diagnosed with a serious illness and Chiara invited both of them, grandmother and Roberta, for a meal. She asked Maria Teresa to put out the best tablecloth "because Jesus is coming to visit us today".

Chiara's grandparents, who lived round the corner, needed someone to stay with them at night. Maria Teresa and Ruggero were exhausted after having spent so many nights away from home, so Chiara offered to take a turn looking after her grandparents. She persisted until eventually her parents agreed to accept her offer. Off she went to her grandparents' house, with a rucksack on her back containing her books for school the next day. She dozed off, but woke up again immediately. She was happy to see that her grandparents were all right and sleeping soundly, but to make sure that she didn't doze off again, she kept pinching her legs. At school no one realised that she hadn't slept that night.

Chiara was full of life. She loved pop music and dancing. She also liked singing; in fact she had a lovely voice. Everybody liked her and she was always surrounded by friends, both girls and boys. "She liked to dress well; she kept her hair well-groomed; and sometimes she wore make-up, but she never overdid it," said one of her friends.

She wanted to be a flight attendant when she grew up. She loved sport, and took every opportunity to do some kind of physical activity. Besides going for long walks in the mountains with her father, collecting mushrooms, Chiara loved tennis and swimming. Maria Teresa recalls her plunging into the huge waves at the seaside time after time.

From Sassello to Savona

In 1985 the Badanos moved to Savona, so that Chiara would be nearer the grammar school. "Everyone else travels daily from Sassello to the city, so why do we have to go and live there?" Chiara asked. But Ruggero's job had moved to Albisola and it was easier for him if they lived in Savona. Anyway they came back to their beloved Sassello every weekend.

Chiara's studies were not going very well, even though she worked hard at school. "She hardly ever went out with her friends," said Maria Teresa, "she really studied hard." But for some reason she didn't seem to hit it off with one female teacher in particular, and she frequently failed the exams. But also in this suffering, Chiara was able to recognise the face of her spouse. She wrote the following to Marita, a friend from the Gen: "They have failed me again, and for me this is a very big suffering. I wasn't able to give this suffering immediately to Jesus. It took me quite a while to accept it and still today, when I think about it, I start crying. It's Jesus forsaken."

Despite her failure at school, Chiara left a trace of light in her teachers and in her classmates. For example, Mr Amoretti, one of her teachers, said: "She put all her trust in the teacher. I remember her gentle smile and the peaceful light in her eyes as she sat in my lessons and those of my colleagues. Of course we had also noticed signs of her spiritual sensitivity and gentleness."

With her parents certain small "adjustments" here and there were required. The time for coming home after being out with her friends, for example, had to be negotiated. Particularly at the weekend, when she was in Sassello, Chiara liked to stay out late. "We were quite concerned," said Maria Teresa, "because she used to stay out late with the boys outside the local café. So we spoke about it and agreed on a time for her to return home. But it wasn't easy. The young people would still be hanging around the café chatting and eating ice cream, while she was sitting at home seething. One day she said: 'I feel like Cinderella who, at midnight, had to run off and who lost her shoe.' We hadn't realised how much this curfew had made her suffer. She would say: 'Don't you trust me?' And we would reply: 'We trust you, yes, but we don't trust the others so much.' Then we came to an agreement: 'All right, so we'll leave it up to you to decide. If, on a particular evening, there is a serious discussion, you might decide to stay. But the next time you should come home at 10.00 o'clock.' She thought about it for a minute and then said: 'That's okay.' In this way we found a balance and she was happy about it."

From Gen 3 to Gen 2

Chiara had something about her that made her different from other young people of her age; it was her ability to be able to immerse herself in the present moment, to "switch off" from things that were not the will of God in that moment. She had an open dialogue with the Lord. In the summer of 1988, just after finding out that she had failed her maths exam, she accompanied a group of Gen 4 to their first international congress in Rome. Her heart was heavy because of the exam result, but it didn't stop her from going. She wrote the following to her parents, from Rome: "An important moment arrived for me: the meeting with Jesus forsaken. It wasn't easy to embrace him; but this morning Chiara Lubich told the Gen 4 that he has to become their spouse." Perhaps Jesus was preparing her for her "big encounter" with him with "pin pricks", as she was to describe it later.

She didn't find the transfer from Gen 3 to Gen 2 so easy either. In fact, many young people find this change a difficult step to take. There are various reasons for this: there are the usual adolescent difficulties; you have to get to know a new group of people, the person in charge changes... But above all, it is the time to make a new choice.

Maria Teresa recalled an important moment when Chiara decided not to go to two Gen 2 meetings in succession. She didn't offer much of an explanation, maybe there was no need: she had to make a personal choice, once again, of the Gospel and of Jesus. Some time later she was asked if she was happy to look after a group of girls in nearby towns who were new to the Focolare and who wanted to live its spirituality. She agreed to do it. This new responsibility, in which she gave herself fully to the others, helped her stop brooding over her own adolescent problems. In this way she came back to the Gen 2, although in effect she had never really left them. She put the whole of herself into following these girls, writing to them and phoning them on a regular basis, and finding small gifts to make them happy...

It was about this time that the first symptoms of the illness appeared. Later she confided to two of the Gen: "The illness arrived just at the right moment, because I was nearly 'lost'; nothing too serious, but our Ideal was becoming secondary... But today you cannot imagine what my relationship with God is like."

Nothing for herself

Chiara always liked to be surrounded by people, by friends. Not that she wasn't capable of being on her own, not at all, but there was something in her that made her go out to others, others who, in a short space of time, would become her friends.

Her closest friends were the Gen boys and girls, with whom she had a simple but profound relationship. One of her Gen friends was Clara "Chicca" Coriasco, who although two years older than Chiara, looked the same age. In fact, they used to enjoy pretending to others that they were twins! Of all Chiara's friends, Chicca was the one with whom she had the closest relationship during adolescence and early adulthood. They would chat for ages on the telephone and write to each other, especially during the period when Chicca was studying in Turin and Chiara was "confined" at Savona. They exchanged the normal kind of chatty letters that one would expect between two young women of their age. Chiara would talk about a gift she had received, about a birthday party she had been to, or about the deep joy she had felt during a Gen meeting. Their correspondence continued and intensified during the brief period of Chiara's illness. Very often it was Chicca who expressed the most intimate spiritual thoughts.

But with the Gen it wasn't just a question of a personal relationship, important though that was. Her Gen unit was a real 'feast' of creative ideas and generosity.

They took every opportunity to "cement their unity" (as they used to say) during their meetings, where they shared their experiences of living the Gospel. And between meetings they would phone each other, write letters, organise trips, send gifts and so on. They lived the communion of goods really seriously. Chiara, for example, right up to her death, kept a list of all her possessions, which she didn't consider to be her personal property. The list was to help make all these things available to anyone who might need them, starting with her Gen friends.

From the many letters that she wrote to the Gen, Chiara comes across as a complete person, someone who communicated her discovery of God-Love and of unity as the ideal of her life. What also emerges is her special love, her passion, for those with no belief in God. Chiara was very active in the Focolare, but particularly so in the newly born Youth for a United World, for which she gave the whole of herself.

In the light of this constant, and continuously renewed communion with the Gen, one can better understand the events of the last two years of Chiara's life. Just a few days before she died she said that, in leaving for heaven she would pass "the torch of unity to those Gen who were left behind". And that is exactly what happened. Still today, Chiara is a model for them. "This is because she fulfilled the ideal that they too have chosen," said Eletta Fornaro, responsible at the time for the Gen girls worldwide. "They want union with God, and she reached it. They want a united world, and she believed in it so much that she was able to bring it about, at least around her, by offering her sufferings. The Gen need concrete examples, and Chiara, even while gravely ill, continued to send her savings to Africa..."

A trail of light

Perhaps Chiara's closest friend in Sassello was Giuliana Robbiano, whose parents owned Bar Gino, where they spent many a happy afternoon or evening. It was there that I spoke to Giuliana. In between serving the customers in the bar, she told me about her relationship with Chiara: "I can honestly say that I spent the most beautiful moments of my life with her," said Giuliana with typical sincerity and simplicity, "Especially during her illness; it was she who kept me going, who knew exactly the right words and the right gestures to give me courage. She was very courteous and polite – everybody liked her. But we never imagined that she had such a rich life. She has left us a trail of light which still today helps me tremendously."

With her friends in Sassello, Chiara Luce never wanted to be the centre of attention. She didn't speak about her Gen experience with them, hers was not an apostolate made up of words – she just loved. "One day I asked her," said Maria Teresa, "'Do you tell your friends in the coffee shop anything about Jesus? Do you try to say something about God?' She replied, quite naturally, 'No, I don't speak to them about God.' I looked at her and said: 'You mean to say you don't take the opportunity to say something?' Chiara replied: 'Talking about God doesn't count for much. I have to give him.'"

Plenty of boys were keen on Chiara, but it didn't go to her head. "She was very balanced with regard to her feelings. She didn't rush into things," explained Chicca, "and she was very clear about her relationships." Chiara was very fond of L., one of the boys from the village. Their relationship lasted no more than a few weeks, before Chiara ended it with him, because she realised that there was something not quite right about the relationship. "She ended it with L. in a very mature, very direct way," said Chicca, "When she told me about it, I could see that she was a very straight person who didn't settle for half measures..." Later, Chiara explained to her mother what had happened: "I was beginning to love L, but I realised that perhaps for him things were different: maybe he just wanted to be with me. So I finished with him."

CHAPTER 3

THE SPOUSE

Then the unexpected happened. It was 1988, summer was coming to an end and the new school year was about to start. The long walks with her friends, the evening discussions, the relaxation time of the holidays were all coming to an end. Chiara was playing tennis one afternoon when she felt a sharp pain in her shoulder. She thought nothing of it, and didn't say anything to her parents or her friends. But it happened again, and this time the pain was sharper, so much so that she couldn't grip the racquet. At first the doctors said that she had cracked a rib, but when the pain did not go away, they decided to investigate further.

Chiara was a bit upset, but she carried on with her life as normal. One afternoon she had planned to go to Genoa for a Gen meeting, but she had a temperature and was in a lot of pain. Later she explained: "The train was at 14.12 and, as there was still plenty of time, I fell asleep. I was woken by the doorbell. There was no one at the door. I looked at my watch and I thought: 'Jesus, it's you who are calling me, do you want me to come to you? I'll have to get the train.' I ran like the wind because I only had seven minutes to get to the station. I was suffering a lot, but I said: 'I have to get there, Jesus is calling me.' I arrived in a sweat and sat down in the train: 'I've made it.'"

The doctors' verdict soon arrived: osteosarcoma with metastasis, one of the most painful and relentless tumours known. Chiara was not told the results of the diagnosis immediately, but she was told that she had a very serious illness. She received the news without flinching. Then there began a series of examinations, periods of waiting, of remission, and of hospitalisation. For Chiara all of this was an opportunity to live the present moment. "In the hospital at Pietra Ligure," Ruggero recalled, "despite the pain and the sickness, she just couldn't stop and rest. She started to help the girl in the next room who was suffering from depression. She would go with this girl wherever she wanted to go, often on long walks round the hospital, although really she should have been resting. When we tried to tell her to be careful she would say: 'I'll be able to sleep later on.'"

Chiara faced up to this trial with an attitude of calm acceptance, "with a smile on her face", you could say. She underwent long periods of treatment, then went back to school for a few days, wrote some letters, spent weeks in bed... "We wrote to each other often," said Chicca Coriasco, "Reading between the lines I had felt for some time that something wasn't quite right, that there was some difficulty. I realised that life had became more difficult for her; also her relationships with others were not as easy. She wanted to be 100% authentic; she wanted to give herself completely... I think that without knowing this, it would be difficult to understand her reaction to the news of her illness."

The spouse draws nearer

The time came for the first operation, followed by a long period of chemotherapy, but Chiara never let it weigh on those around her. In this regard Maria Teresa recalled a decisive moment in Chiara's life, a rather extraordinary episode: "For some time she had realised that things were going badly and that she really did have cancer. Nevertheless she was full of hope that she would be cured. A few days after the operation she asked the doctor what the real prognosis was. So she discovered the truth about her illness and she was also told that she would lose her hair through the chemotherapy. In fact, it was probably this that made her realise the gravity of the illness: she was quite proud of her hair. We were in Turin staying with friends, because the operation had been done in the Regina Margherita hospital there. I can still see her there in the garden in her green coat. She had a fixed, almost absent look on her face as she came into the house. I asked her how it had gone and she replied: 'Not now, don't let's talk about it now.' She threw herself down on the bed, her eyes closed and stayed there for twenty-five minutes. I was dying inside, but the only thing to do was to stay beside her, in silence, suffering with her. It was a battle. Eventually she turned towards me, smiling: 'Now we can talk,' she said. It was done. She had said her 'yes' once again, and she never turned back from that. (Only once did she ask the reason for her suffering. After the first operation she had exclaimed: 'Why, Jesus?' But a few moments later she said: 'If you want it Jesus, then so do I.')"

Chiara wrote to Chiara Lubich: "Jesus has sent me this illness just at the right moment. He sent it to me so that I could find him again." That smile which had always been her hallmark, and which had never left her face during the first few months of the illness, returned more radiant than ever. Chiara knew now where she was going.

Operations and aspirations

The course of the illness was merciless, although Chiara was determined to lead a normal life and to live joyfully, because the relationship with her spouse was growing. She had a second, very painful operation.

Of the many experiences lived in this period, one is particularly striking. It happened during what turned out to be Chiara's last Christmas (she herself thought it would be her last one). She had prepared all the presents for her family and friends. For Chiara it was very important to celebrate Christmas surrounded by the people she loved. But things started to get rapidly worse. "The doctor asked me a number of pointed questions," said Maria Teresa, "and wanted to know how long it would take to get her to the hospital in Turin. The ambulance arrived, but Chiara didn't want to go: 'I am not spending Christmas in hospital,' she said, 'If I have to die, Jesus, I want to die at home.' I whispered in her ear that it was the will of God to go. She accepted it, but she didn't utter a word during the journey; she was suffering terribly. When we arrived at the hospital, the doctors, who thought the world of her, were waiting there, ready to do the blood transfusion. We were in danger of losing her."

"The next morning, which was Christmas Eve," Maria Teresa recalled, "I went into her room and said: 'Everybody's running around with piles of presents, but no one looks you in the eyes, no one passes the time of day. Jesus is next to them and they don't see him.' In the meantime Chiara had just come through a very difficult patch. I continued: 'Let's light the fire of Jesus in our midst, so that he will warm everyone. You'll have to light it, because my wood doesn't give off much heat.' 'Let's do it together,' Chiara replied."

That very afternoon Cardinal Saldarini of Turin was visiting the ward. He was struck by Chiara's face. He said: "You have a marvellous light in your eyes. How come?" After a moment's hesitation Chiara replied: "I try to love Jesus."

Also on that same day, one of the hospital volunteer workers had a deep personal crisis: "How can God exist when children are dying of cancer in this hospital?" While Maria Teresa was making her way down to the café, the lady sat down by Chiara. We don't know what passed between them, but that woman now says that it was the most beautiful Christmas of her life. "We all felt the same, " echoed Ruggero.

Close to her friends

The Gen girls and boys were always there, at the ready, to help Chiara's family in any way possible. They all had more or less the same experience. "To start with we all thought that we were going there to support her," said Fernando Garetto, a Gen from Turin, "But we soon realised that we couldn't do without her, it was if we were drawn by a magnet. Every time we went into her room," he continued, "we felt that we had to 'adjust' our souls; and then we were filled with joy in those brief moments spent with her. It felt as if we were being projected, without any merit on our part, into her splendid adventure of love with God. And yet Chiara didn't come out with any extraordinary words, nor did she write pages and pages in her diary. She just loved." One of her doctors, Antonio Delogu, explained the possible reason for the joy which she radiated: "She showed with her smile, with her big luminous eyes, that death doesn't exist – only life exists." But it wasn't all one-way traffic. Chiara wrote this to the Gen of Genoa: "I feel your unity very strongly, your offerings, your prayers which allow me to renew my 'yes', moment by moment."

Ruggero explained it like this: "We saw the hand of God in the illness. I discovered a new family that I didn't realise I had. And Chiara's relationship with

Jesus helped us take the necessary spiritual steps ahead. She communicated serenity to us: Chiara was desperately ill, and yet we never fell into despair, because in her there was always Jesus. I remember one occasion when we had done meditation together. Chiara said: 'When we have Jesus present in our midst, we are the happiest family in the world.' And that night she started singing some of the Gen songs, so much so that I was afraid she might disturb the neighbours. But I didn't dare interrupt her."

Roberto Bertucci, who wrote the first biography of Chiara, emphasised "the unusual relationship she had built with her parents. It was a relationship of great harmony and of the deepest unity. Immediately after Chiara had gone to heaven, Ruggero said: 'God gave her to us and he has taken her back. Blessed be God. I don't know if we will be able to do anything else in this life, but maybe we have made at least one masterpiece.' It says something about the faith of Chiara's parents and the great fruits that can come from a good Christian family."

Another of Chiara's friends, Gianfranco Piccardo, was going off on a humanitarian mission to the African state of Benin, to dig wells for drinking water. Chiara gave him all of her savings, almost £700, money she had received on her last birthday. "I don't need it," she said, "I've got everything." She was already confined to bed, paralysed. Gianfranco's wife, Rosalba, visited Chiara regularly and kept her up to date on the project. Rosalba recalled the last time she saw Chiara: "In that last handshake it felt as if the immense love of a creature who was totally in God was being passed on to me."

The beautiful lady

There is a tape recording in which Chiara speaks about a visit she received when she was in hospital having injections between the vertebrae to stop the terrible contractions she was getting in her legs, even though they had been paralysed for some time already. She recorded it for the Gen, saying; "It is very important at this moment to keep Jesus in the midst, and so I wanted to tell you an experience I had in Turin, where I had gone to see the specialist. I was very afraid, because I had no idea what they were going to do to me. They said that I was going to have a little operation under a local anaesthetic. It was a really beautiful experience, because just as they started this little operation, someone came to visit me. It was a beautiful lady with a radiant smile. She came right up to me, took my hand and told me to be brave. I was convinced she was someone from the Movement, because that light that she radiated was from our Ideal. I thought that my parents, who were waiting outside, had let her in. Then, just as quickly as she had appeared, she disappeared, and I never saw her again. But I was filled with a very great joy and all my fears went away. When I came out of the theatre, I asked my parents who the lady was, but they didn't know her. Now, looking back over it, I haven't got an explanation for what happened, but I felt very strongly that I had to thank God. Thinking rationally I thought: 'It was just a coincidence.' But then I asked myself: 'why did she arrive right at that moment, in that situation? And above all with that light, which without exaggerating, I would say was supernatural.' She was like an angel – an angel that Our Lady put next to me. It was a very profound moment of God. In that moment I understood something: if we were always ready for everything, how many signs God would send us! I also understood just how many times God passes near us and we don't realise it.'

No morphine

The various treatments turned out to be ineffective and the cancer continued to grow. "If I had to choose between being able to walk and going to heaven, I would choose heaven," Chiara said on one occasion, "That's all that interests me... I am wary about saying it because maybe they'll think I want to go there so as not to suffer any more. But that's not why. I want to go to Jesus."

The last CAT scan left her with no hope of a cure. These were to be her last few months, the most intense ones. Numerous witnesses tell us how Chiara, from her sick bed, lived in communion with many people. So much so that Chiara's doctors started to become curious as they observed her and her parents. "We watched them very carefully," commented a doctor from the Regina Margherita hospital, "because we couldn't understand why they weren't desperate. There were three of them, but we saw only one person."

Maria Teresa recalled another episode: "Her veins were a mess because of all the injections and drips she had had. The consultant sent the best nurse to try to find a good vein. She was having great difficulty, but she wouldn't give up. Eventually she found a vein in Chiara's thumb that was still all right. It was a very small one and could easily break at any moment. She said to Chiara: 'You'll have to help me by keeping still. If you move your thumb at all, the needle will come out and we can't give you the treatment.' A butterfly needle was inserted. For three days Chiara kept perfectly still. One evening she said: 'For me this is a little trial. It hurts and I am sorely tempted to move my thumb. So, to overcome this temptation I say that this butterfly neddle is one of the thorns that Jesus had in his head.'"

She even refused morphine: "It takes away my lucidity, and all I have to offer Jesus is suffering. That's all I've got left. If I'm not lucid, what sense has my life got?"

Her room

Chiara spent almost the whole of the last few months of her life in her bedroom at Sassello, looked after by her parents and by her Aunt Mimma, a real angel of serenity and dedication. Chiara loved that little room, with its wooden beams and with two windows. One of these was a French window that looked out on to the garden; the other, right opposite her bed, looked up at the sky and always had two vases of beautiful flowers on the ledge. Distributed round the room were twenty or so rag dolls which the Gen 4 had given her, and which Chiara really loved. Then there was a picture of Jesus forsaken on the cross underneath which was written: "Jesus I trust in you." There was also a picture of Saint-Exupéry's Little Prince, under which was written: "You only see well with your heart, the essential things are invisible to the eyes."

By her bed was the telephone with which Chiara kept in contact with her friends. Although totally immobile, Chiara was highly active. She followed all the activities of the Gen and made her presence felt through postcards, messages and little gifts. She always managed to find a way to show her unity. And she continued to have a special love for those who did not believe in God. Fabio De Marzi, one of her doctors, an agnostic, and someone who had been many times to visit Chiara, recalled: "From when I got to know Chiara and her parents, something within me changed. They were people who were completely coherent and I understood what Christianity was."

There was also a small statue of St Clare, a pair of little girl's shoes, an oil lamp made from a sardine tin, a little figure of Our Lady of Fatima and a picture of a red sunset. On a pencil case was printed the following quotation from Chiara Lubich: "Love, love always, love everyone. At the end of every day we should be able to say: 'I have always loved'."

Then there were the books, lots and lots of books, from Dostoevsky to Dante, from Agatha Christie to Rudyard Kipling. Her favourites were *Meditations* and *Conversations with the Gen* by Chiara Lubich. Finally, there was a computer print out in large block capitals: "Ciao Chiara, 1". The Gen were constantly with Chiara, even when her suffering was at its worst.

Heaven's door

Chiara also went through a moment of great trial. One day her mother heard her shout out loud. She ran in to the room straightaway to find her gasping for breath and covered in sweat. "Mum, the devil came in here," said Chiara. Maria Teresa tried to calm her, telling her not to be too surprised by such a visit, "because the devil wants to take the most beautiful souls for himself. Jesus is with you." Chiara regained her peace and continued on her holy journey.

Chiara was mature far beyond her eighteen years. Dr Fabio De Marzi wrote this to her: "I'm not used to seeing young people like you. I have always regarded your age as one of great emotion, intense joy and wild enthusiasm. But you have taught me that it's also a time of total maturity."

On 19 July 1989 Chiara started haemorrhaging terribly and they were only just able to save her. She said: "Don't shed tears for me. I'm going to Jesus, to start another life. I don't want people crying at my funeral; I want joyful singing. Yesterday I was at heaven's door, but it wasn't open."

Other treatments followed, including a very difficult blood transfusion: "Every drop is a little like the blows of the hammer on the nails used to crucify Jesus," said Chiara. With each pulse of the machine she said: "For you."

On one particular occasion she asked her parents not to let Giuliano and her other friends come into her room. Some time later she explained why: "It wasn't a sign of sadness or because I felt less for you, on the contrary. It was just that it was difficult to come down from the marvellous place where my soul was living, to then go back up again. I am living in another dimension, in an atmosphere of paradise which has enraptured me, and everything that takes me away from there feels like dead-wood."

Those who were near Chiara also experienced this "atmosphere of paradise". She was reaching the final stage of the journey. Those who saw her during this period testify to the fact that she was always at peace, even though she was suffering terribly. She had difficulty speaking, she could hardly write, but she was completely immersed in the will of God of the present moment.

Spiritual intimacy

It was during the last few months of her life that Chiara Badano's relationship with Chiara Lubich reached a deeper level. We can see this from the exchange of letters between them.

On 20 December 1989 Chiara Badano wrote: "Two days ago I came back to the hospital in Turin where, over the last ten months or so, I have been umpteen times for chemotherapy. My current state of health is not the greatest, because my body has been battered by the various treatments I've had. The last time I came here coincided with the Gen 2 congress at Castelgandolfo. One morning I was feeling particularly ill. I knew that that was the day when the Gen were going to be praying specially for me. I too felt the desire to be united with them and so Mum and I prayed together. As this year is the year of the Holy Spirit, besides asking to be cured I asked the Eternal Father to illuminate the organisers of the congress with his Spirit, and I asked for wisdom and light for all the Gen. It really was a moment of God: I was suffering a lot physically, but my soul was singing. Now I would like to ask you for a Christmas present: a Word of Life for me, one for dad and one for mum. Am I asking too much?"

Chiara Lubich replied by return of post: "You will probably have heard that the Gen congress was a real manifestation of the Holy Spirit, thanks also to you. I can sense that you are totally committed to doing the will of God and to offering him your continued 'yes' for the Movement. I am with you constantly with my prayers and with all my love. I have chosen the Words of Life you asked for. Yours is: 'Those who abide in me and I in them bear much fruit' (Jn 15: 5). I propose this one for your mum: 'Rejoice in hope, be patient in suffering, persevere in prayer' (Rm. 12: 12). And for your dad: 'I love you, O Lord, my strength. The Lord is my rock, my fortress and my deliverer' (Ps. 18, 1-2). I am asking the Holy Spirit to give you the gift of fortitude, so that your soul, through love for Jesus forsaken, will always be able to 'sing'."

In April 1990, while she continued her Calvary, Chiara was reading the Word of Life of the month, with a commentary written by Chiara Lubich. She underlined one particular passage: "The first condition for overcoming a trial is vigilance. We must understand that these trials, which are permitted by God, are not sent to discourage us, but so that, by overcoming them, we can mature spiritually."

On 19 July 1990, Chiara wrote another letter to Chiara Lubich: "First of all I want to update you about the state of my health. They have stopped giving me the chemotherapy because it was no use. So, medicine has laid down its arms! Now only God can do anything. Stopping the therapy has meant an increase in the back pain, and I am hardly able to turn on to my side.

"This evening my heart is full of joy. Do you know why? Carlo Grisolia's mum came from Genoa to see me (Carlo was a Gen who had died some time ago). It was a very strong moment of Jesus in the midst. I was so moved that I found it almost impossible to speak.

She brought me some photos of Carlo so that I could choose one for myself. In fact I have it right in front of me now. While I was with his mother, Carlo was also with us. In fact, his presence was so strong that I found myself looking at the chair in my room to see if he really was there. Yes, he was there!

"Oh Mammina, will I manage to be faithful to Jesus forsaken and live to meet him, like Carlo did? I feel so small and the road ahead is so hard. Often I feel overwhelmed by suffering. But it's my spouse who is coming to visit me, right? Yes, I will repeat, with you, 'If you want it, Jesus, I want it too.' Another thing I wanted to say: here everyone is praying for a miracle (and you know how much I would like that…), but I am not able to ask for one. Perhaps I find it difficult to ask for a miracle because I feel that it is not in his will. Could that be so? What do you think?

"I would be happy if you could choose a new name for me (if you think it the right moment)."

A week later the reply arrived: "Thanks for your letter in which you tell me about your health and the visit from Carlo's mum. Jesus in the midst that you established with her was so great that you also felt the presence of Carlo. I am happy about that. Thanks too for your photo. Your luminous face shows your love for Jesus. Chiara, don't be afraid to say your 'yes' to him moment by moment. He will give you strength, be sure of it! I too am praying for this and am always there with you. God loves you immensely. He wants to penetrate the most intimate part of your soul to give you a little taste of heaven.

"The name I have thought of for you is Chiara Luce. Do you like it? It is the light of the Ideal which conquers the world. I send it with all my love. On St Clare's feast day you too will be with me, spiritually."

On 9 August of that year, Chiara Luce wrote her last affectionate letter, signing it with her new name. She sends her greetings for the feast of St Clare: "I wanted to send you a basket full of mushrooms from Sassello, but despite my efforts, as you will have seen, we only managed to find one: I think it was made just for you. I am with you and I am offering everything, my failures, the sufferings and the joys, to him, starting again every time I feel the weight of the cross. As I can't fit into the basket to greet you personally, I am doing it in writing."

Why has Jesus still not come for me?

One day, as she was nearing the end of her Holy Journey, she said: "I can't wait to go to paradise… But perhaps this too is an attachment, something I have to lose." She was afraid that some people had put her "on a pedestal". She wrote: "Jesus has allowed this trial, but the merit is his if I manage to accept it… I have very little to do with it."

By now she was certain that there would be no miracle cure, and she was happy about it. So together with her mother and the Gen girls, she started to prepare her "wedding reception", that is, her funeral, in every detail. She said that she wanted to wear a white dress with a pink belt, and she asked Chicca to try it on for her. Then she chose the music, the songs and the readings. You could say that these last days of her life, when she was paralysed and in continuous need of oxygen, were the last period of her engagement, before "the wedding", as she used to say.

Chiara Luce was lucid right to the end. She constantly refused to take any painkillers that might have reduced her capacity to think and express herself clearly. During those last few days, she also had plenty of advice for her parents. "Mum, while I am getting ready on my death bed," she said, "you must keep repeating: 'Now Chiara Luce can see Jesus.'"

After her death, a barely legible note written by Chiara, was discovered. It said: "Holy Christmas 1990. Thank you for everything! Happy New Year." She had hidden it in a drawer amongst the greetings cards, in the knowledge that her mother would have found it next Christmas, after Chiara Luce had gone to heaven.

Her dad asked her if she was still happy to donate her corneas, the only organs left in her body that were not affected by the cancer or by the chemotherapy. She responded with a brilliant smile.

With great difficulty she wrote a kind of testimony for the Gen: "I have gone out of your life in an instant. Oh how I would have loved to stop that train which was taking me further and further away! But I still didn't understand. I was still too full with so many ambitions, projects and who knows what (things that now seem so unimportant, futile and passing). Another world was waiting for me, and all I had to do was abandon myself to it. But now I feel enveloped in a splendid plan which is being revealed to me little by little."

"I owe everything to God and to Chiara," was one of her very last sentences.

The wedding

Chiara Luce began to decline rapidly. Breathing had become extremely difficult and there were signs she might suffocate. One morning she confided to her mother: "Do you think it is a false alarm? Am I really about to go?" "You only leave in God's time," said Maria Teresa. "But rest assured, your suitcase is ready, full of acts of love." "Do you think I will meet Grandma there?" asked Chiara. "You will see Mary first," replied Maria Teresa, "who will welcome you with open arms." "Be quiet," answered Chiara Luce, "don't spoil the surprise."

Two nights before she died Chiara Luce asked her mother to read her one of Chiara Lubich's meditations. Maria Teresa started reading, but Chiara Luce stopped her: "More enthusiasm, please," she said. Then suddenly Chiara Luce spoke out strongly, it was something referring to the "visit" she had had a few weeks before: "When the devil comes I send him away, because I am stronger, because I have Jesus."

On the eve of her departure for paradise she wanted to say goodbye to the friends who were in the house. She had hardly any strength left, but she managed to give a smile to each one, or to make a sign with her hand. One of those present that evening was Giuliano. Chiara Luce somehow found the strength to say to him: "You must have the courage to put aside ambitions and plans that destroy the true meaning of life, which is to believe in the love of God, and nothing else." When a beautiful bouquet of roses arrived from the Gen, Chiara commented: "They're lovely – just right for a wedding."

She had started that morning to repeat an expression recommended by Chiara Lubich: "Come Lord Jesus," because she wanted to receive the Eucharist. Then, quite unexpectedly, a priest arrived and gave her Communion. She was so happy.

That night, it was not easy for Chiara Luce. The doctors were doing their best to help, but Chiara asked to be left alone with her parents and friends. Right next to her were her mother and father; outside, in the corridor, were the Gen and other friends. There was an atmosphere of peace, of normality almost. She spoke her last words to her mother: "Ciao. Be happy, because I am." When Ruggero asked her if those words also applied to him, she squeezed his hand. It was 4.00 on the morning of Sunday 7 October 1990. Chiara Luce had arrived.

Chiara Lubich sent the following message in a telegram to Ruggero and Maria Teresa: "We thank God for this, his luminous masterpiece." Then the final gift: her corneas were removed. Now, thanks to Chiara Luce, two young people can see again.

CHAPTER 4

THE CELEBRATION CONTINUES

The news of Chiara Luce's death had spread round Sassello before dawn had broken. That morning saw a procession of people going up to the Badanos' house - and they weren't just people from Sassello. They came from Savona, Genoa, Turin and from places even further afield.

"She's made it," was what people were saying as they queued to go into the room where Chiara Luce was lying, dressed in her wedding gown. There was no sadness, although there were plenty of tears. People were reciting the Rosary continuously, and everyone was joining in: relatives, focolarini, parishioners, people who never darkened the doors of the church... Chiara Luce belonged to all of them – no one was excluded. There was a real atmosphere of celebration, so much so that one child asked his mother when the cakes were arriving!

On Tuesday 9 October, by special request of the mayor of Sassello, all the shops stayed shut. More than two thousand people came to the funeral, which was held in the parish church of the Most Holy

Trinity. In fact, more than half the people had to stay outside on the piazza. In that same piazza there is a sundial which had stimulated Chiara Luce to write the following, in one of her last pieces of schoolwork: "Often man does not live his life, because he is immersed in times that do not exist: things that happened in the past, or which he now regrets. Man could give meaning to everything by leaving his selfishness behind and going out to others."

The undertaker had never seen a funeral like this one. His mother said she didn't want to see Chiara Luce's body – she wanted to remember her as she was when she was alive. But he convinced her to go, "You will see the body of a saint there," he said.

There were so many people there that when one of Chiara Luce's friends fainted, the crowd was so tightly packed that she remained upright. Maria Teresa and Ruggero managed to sing, as Chiara had asked, despite all the emotion. She had said to them: "You must sing, because I will be singing with you." And they repeated time and again what Chiara had recommended them to say: "Now Chiara Luce can see Jesus."

Those present remarked on the atmosphere of paradise, of joy, of making a choice of God, because of Chiara Luce's choice of God. One of her friends commented: "For the first time I was certain of the love of God." And another friend said: "You, who like me, had dreams, hopes and illusions, help me to make my life into a masterpiece." One of the Gen girls said: "Many things unite us: congresses, meetings, songs, experiences, dances, laughing together... But there is something else I would like to do together with Chiara Luce: become a saint." Many of those present underwent a real change in their lives.

Bishop Maritano, who was very moved during the mass, said in his homily: "This is the fruit of a Christian family, of a community of Christians, the result of a Movement that lives mutual love and has Jesus in the midst." He acknowledged the greatness of Chiara Luce's witness, "a witness of faith which has transformed these two years of suffering, of terrible physical suffering; but what transforms, what makes the miracle, is love."

One of the bidding prayers at the funeral mass was: "That all of us may meet God as Chiara has met him and has testified: as love."

Why Chiara Luce?

Chiara Luce's fame began to spread, slowly but surely. The account of her funeral passed from mouth to mouth, bouncing like a skimming stone across a lake. Her letters, her words and photographs were circulating in the diocese, in the Focolares and amongst those who knew her. Eventually, the bishop of Acqui Terme, Livio Maritano, decided to open the diocesan process of canonisation which, if all goes well, is followed by that conducted by the Holy See in Rome. Chiara Luce was beatified on 25 September 2010.

Bishop Maritano explained why he had taken the cause of Chiara Luce to heart: "It seemed to me that her witness was of particular significance for young people. Just think about how she lived her illness and the effect her death has had on people. You can't ignore such an important example. There is a need for sanctity today, as always. People need help to find a direction, to have an aim in life. Young people need help to overcome insecurity, loneliness, a sense of failure, suffering, death and everything that disturbs their peace. Theoretical discussions don't win them over – they need witnesses.

"In the conversations I had with her," continued the bishop, "I saw a maturity much greater that that of most young people of her age. She had understood the essence of Christianity: God in the first place, Jesus, with whom she had a spontaneous, sisterly, relationship; Mary as a model; the centrality of love; the responsibility of proclaiming the Gospel, something that she did very effectively with her life. All this, tempered by the experience of suffering and death, not feared but welcomed, makes her whole story quite unique."

Asked what he saw as the effects of the Focolare spirituality on Chiara Luce's life, Bishop Maritano said: "I think that key points of the Focolare spirituality, God is love, unity and a passion for the Church, were all present in Chiara Luce. Certainly the Church owes thanks to Chiara Lubich, because her Movement had an enormous influence on the spiritual formation of young Badano."

Bishop Maritano's secretary, Mariagrazia Magrini, was chosen to be vice-postulator by the Congregation for the causes of saints. She couldn't hide her enthusiasm for what she considers to be "not a bureaucratic task, but a sensitive role". She has been working very hard for several years now, and it seems that her efforts are bearing fruit. "I took on the task of collecting writings by and to Chiara Luce," she explained, "including those that have come to light since her death. But above all, besides drawing up a list of witnesses, I am trying to bring out what Chiara Luce really is: a saint of our times. The more I find out about her, the more convinced I become of this. Even the letters she wrote as a little girl show her as someone who really loved Jesus. Other things that emerge are her love for others, forgetting herself, her joy for living and giving and her joy in looking forward to her death."

Thirteen years on

When you go to visit the cemetery in Sassello it's not difficult to find Chiara Luce's grave. You can tell by the way the grass is worn, by the large number of people making their way to the Badanos' chapel. There, a photograph of her smiling face welcomes the visitor. Still, on 7 October every year, a large number of people gather together to remember her. Above all, it is the young people who find in her life a meaning for their lives. They like the way she lived her faith, which was at the same time both normal and radical. They like the fact that she was a modern young woman with whom they can identify. They feel that she is one of them, and that she managed to remain faithful to God right to the end.

Very often visitors leave a message next to her photo. Some express their thanks to Chiara Luce for a grace received, some are grateful for her friendship. Others are asking her to pray for a sick person or entrust their own soul to her.

Chiara Luce's experience is contagious. A young girl who is seriously ill and undergoing dialysis, wrote, during a Gen congress: "God showed me that Chiara Luce is my model. I want to declare my 'yes' to Jesus forsaken, in front of everyone."

Others felt the need to share their possessions. The Giribaldi family, for example, have a cottage in the mountains. They decided to name it after Chiara Luce and offer it to those who could not otherwise afford a holiday.

Then there are those who give money for "Project Africa", as Chiara had done with her savings. After her death an envelope was found containing 70,000 lire (£35) on which was written "For Africa". Since then more than £50,000 has been collected and sent to Benin, where it has been distributed by the Focolare community there. A whole chapter could be written on this subject alone, but one moving story will have to suffice. Two Gen from Benin had received some of this money with which to buy food, but they felt that they couldn't keep it all for themselves. So they bought a bottle of bleach and went to clean the bathroom of their next-door neighbour who suffers from leprosy.

Chiara Luce's story spread far and wide through the media. Maria, a thirteen-year-old girl from Sassari, in Sardinia, read about her in the Focolare magazine *Città Nuova*. The next day she took it to school with her and asked her Italian teacher if she could read it out to the whole class: "After asking for God's help, I asked the teacher if I could read it to the class. I couldn't believe it when she said yes. I was very nervous when I got up in front of my classmates, but when I started to speak I felt confident because I realised that that story would bring joy and help to many people. The comments were very positive and now some of my classmates are beginning to believe in our ideal of unity."

Chiara Luce has also helped bring out vocations, like that of George Dobrescu, a twenty-six-year-old Romanian. He never met Chiara Luce but, he says, he became her "brother". For a number of years he had been staying with the Badanos while he was studying. "Living in Chiara's world," he said, "I received a great light and it changed me. She was my sister. I spent a lot of time in the chapel at the cemetery. In fact, one day I actually nodded off… but it is through her that I found the most important thing in my life: my vocation as a focolarino."

Another person rediscovered his vocation when he read about Chiara Luce in *Città Nuova*. He was a 28-year-old priest belonging to a religious order. "I happened to pick up a copy of *Città Nuova*," he explained,

"I read Chiara Luce's story. And then I re-read it. I was in crisis about my vocation at the time and her story was a great example for me. Like me, she had chosen Jesus, but she remained faithful to her choice, right to the end, not like me. But I want to start again with the help and the prayers of Chiara Luce."

A generation of saints

In one of her world-wide telephone link-ups with members of the Movement, Chiara Lubich spoke about Chiara Luce: "In one of her last letters Chiara Luce told me of her decision to want to love Jesus forsaken for himself, not so that she could get some benefit for herself. She wanted to love suffering for his sake, for Jesus forsaken, and not because of the divine alchemy which, as we know, transforms suffering into love. And Chiara Luce certainly knew what suffering was, especially during the last few months of her earthly life. But she had understood that these sufferings were precious pearls which had to be gathered lovingly every day. It was especially in the sufferings that required fortitude, patience, perseverance and constancy... that she felt able to love. It was in the "surprises", as she called the frequent physical sufferings, that she was able to meet him, to see his face, disfigured and yet loving, and embrace him... So, she lived with him, and with him she transformed her passion into a wedding hymn."

NEW CITY PRESS

Hyde Park, New York
www.newcitypress.com

New City Press is one of more than 20 publishing houses sponsored by the Focolare, a movement founded by Chiara Lubich to help bring about the realization of Jesus' prayer: "That all may be one" (John 17:21). In view of that goal, New City Press publishes books and resources that enrich the lives of people and help all to strive toward the unity of the entire human family. We are a member of the Association of Catholic Publishers.

Also from New City Press

Chiara Badano (DVD); Maria A. Calo
978-1-56548-424-5 $15.95
Filmed on location in Italy, this powerful film tells the story of Blessed Chiara Badano from her childhood to her beatification in 2010.

15 Days of Prayer with Blessed Chiara Badano;
Florence Gillet 978-1-56548-554-9 $12.95
This very young woman, a person of our own times, bore witness above all to the beauty of being a disciple of Christ.

World of GeeBee & W (DVD); Walter Kostner
978-1-56548-252-4 $5.95
With lovable clown-like faces, these two pals discover some of life's most valuable lessons all in a days' play.

Gospel for Children; John J. Piantedosi & Ben
Cioffi (Illustrator) 978-1-56548-370-5 $13.95
Introduces preschool and middle-school-aged children to Jesus through the major events in his life.

New Horizons; Chiara Amirante
978-1-90503-910-4 $14.95
It is a novel, a thriller and a love story, but above all it is a beacon of hope in our broken society.

Realizarse a los 18; Michele Zanzucchi
978-9-50586-253-5 $13.50
Vida y huella de Chiara "Luce" Badano.